Kim Naps

by Carmel Reilly

illustrated by Ruth Bennett

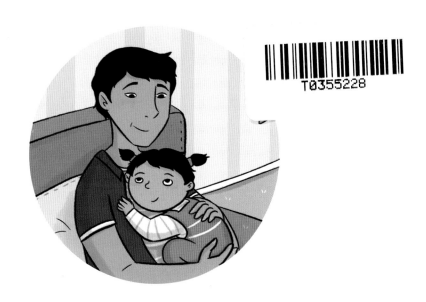

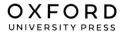

OXFORD
UNIVERSITY PRESS

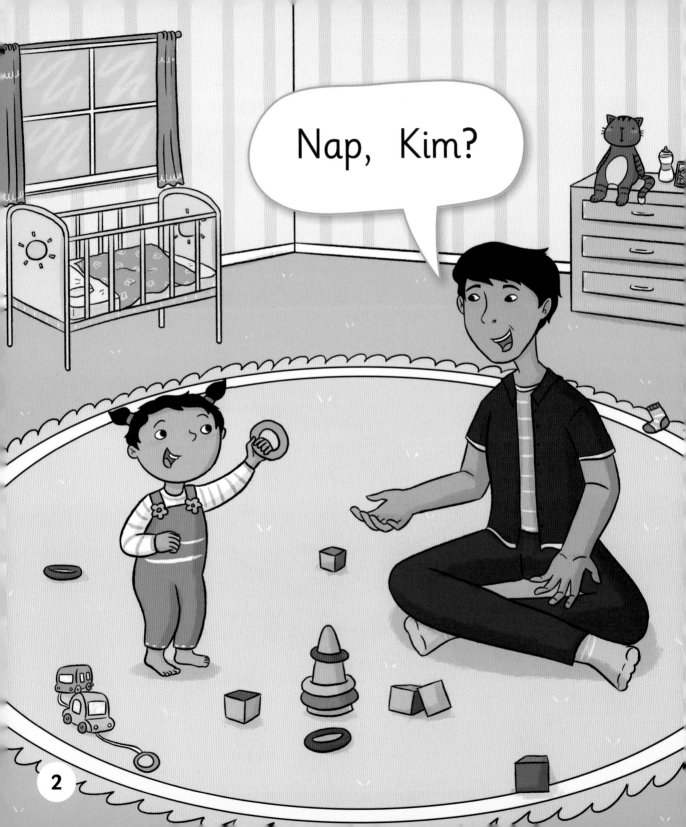

Dad put Kim in the cot.

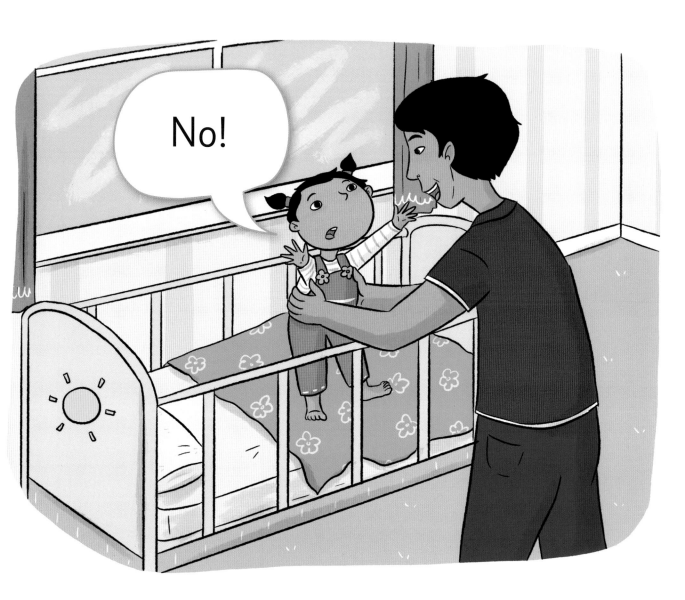

Kim sat in the cot.

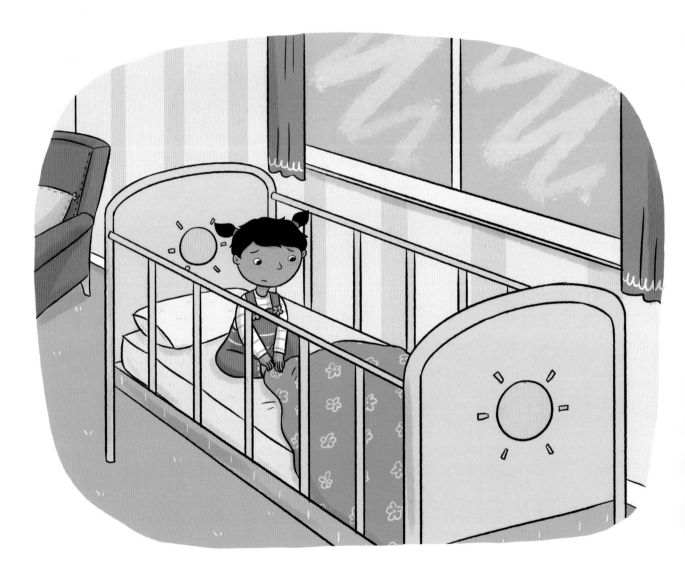

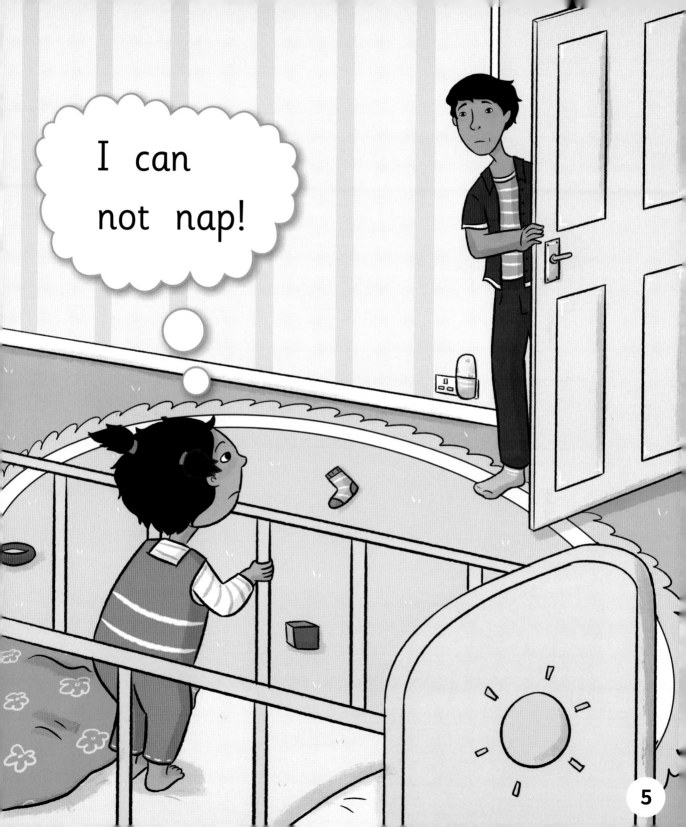

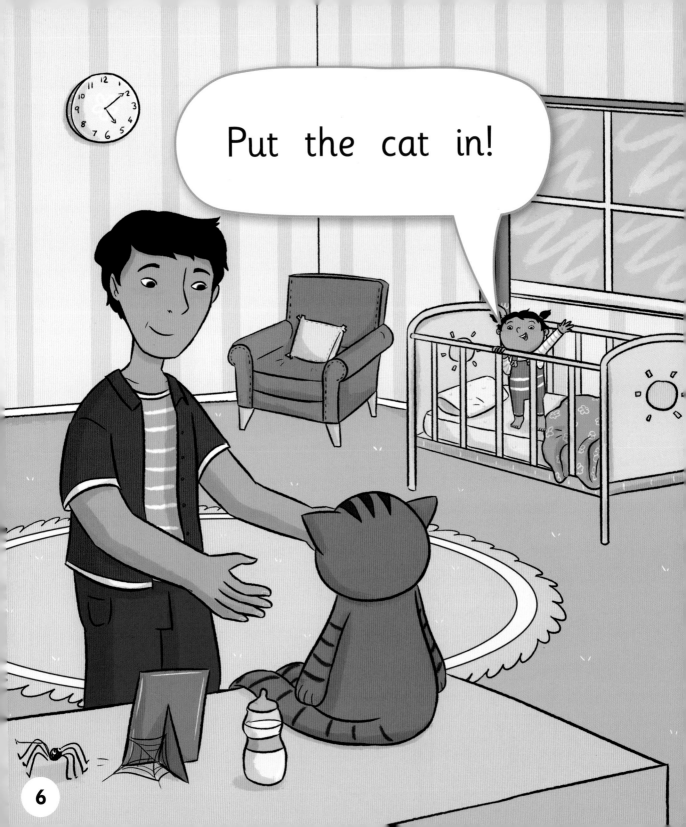

6

Dad got the cat.

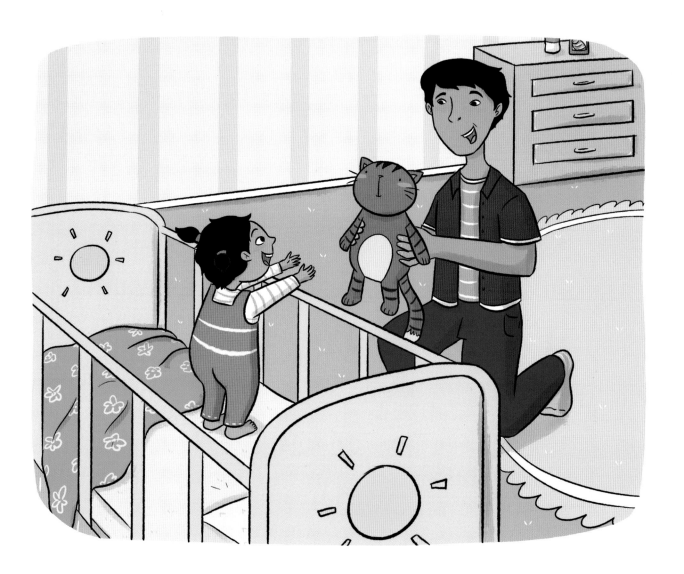

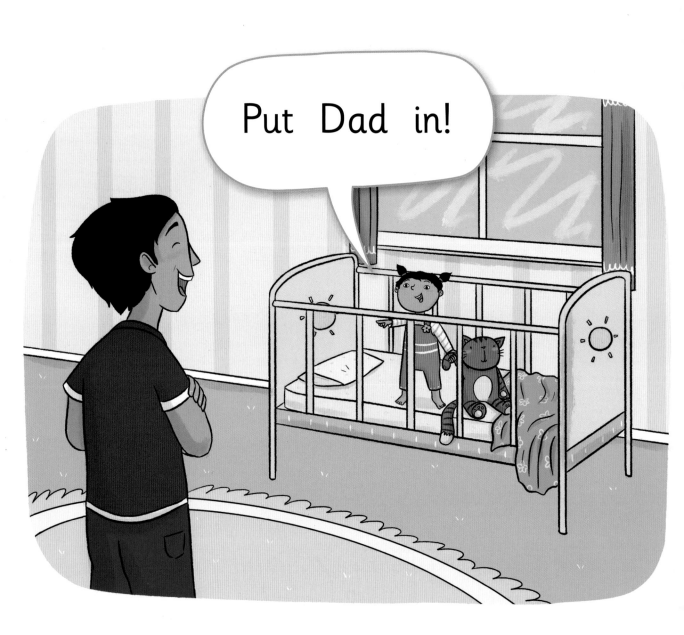

Dad got in the cot.

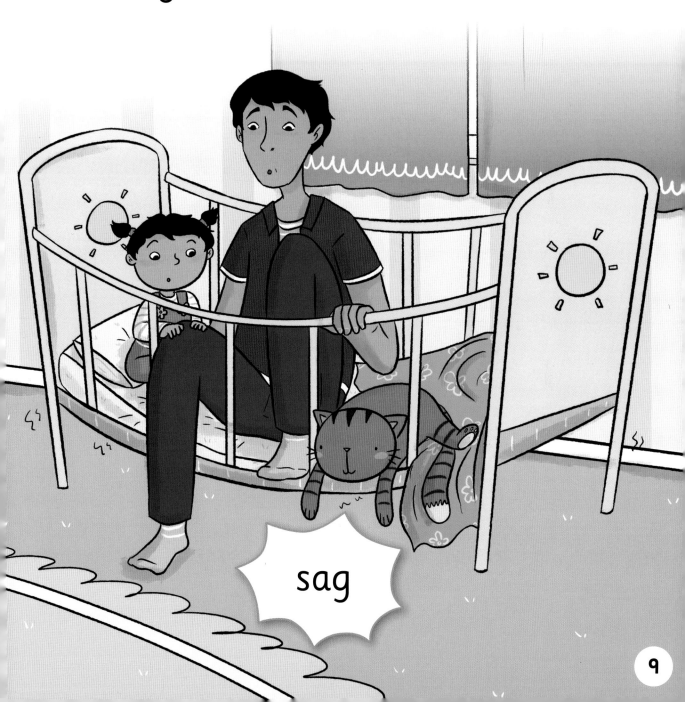

Kim sat on Dad.

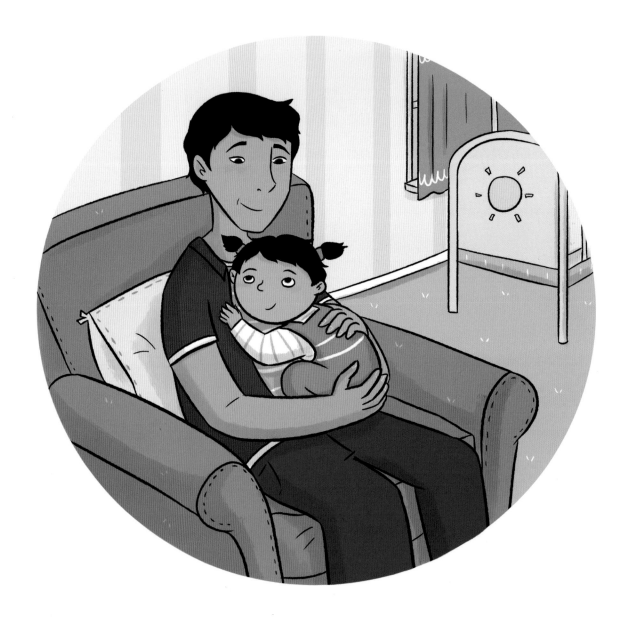

The cat sat on Kim.

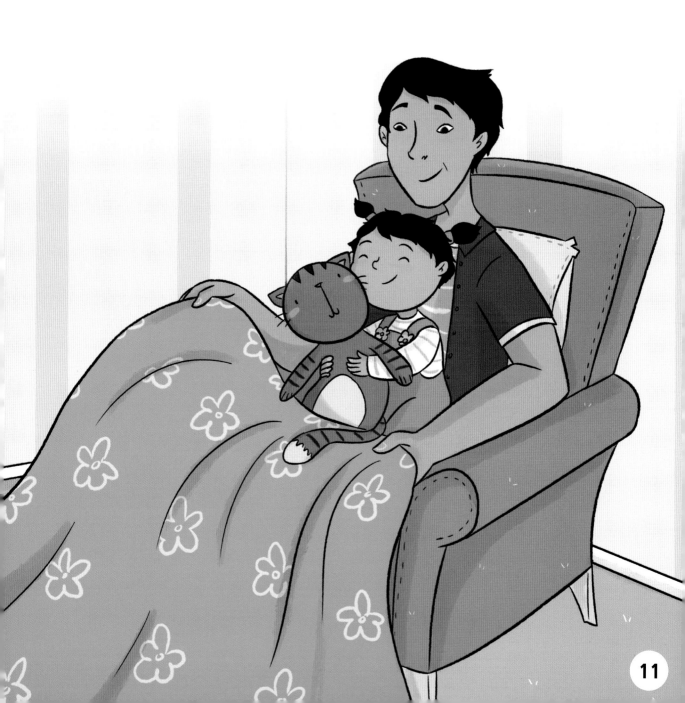

Kim and Dad nap.

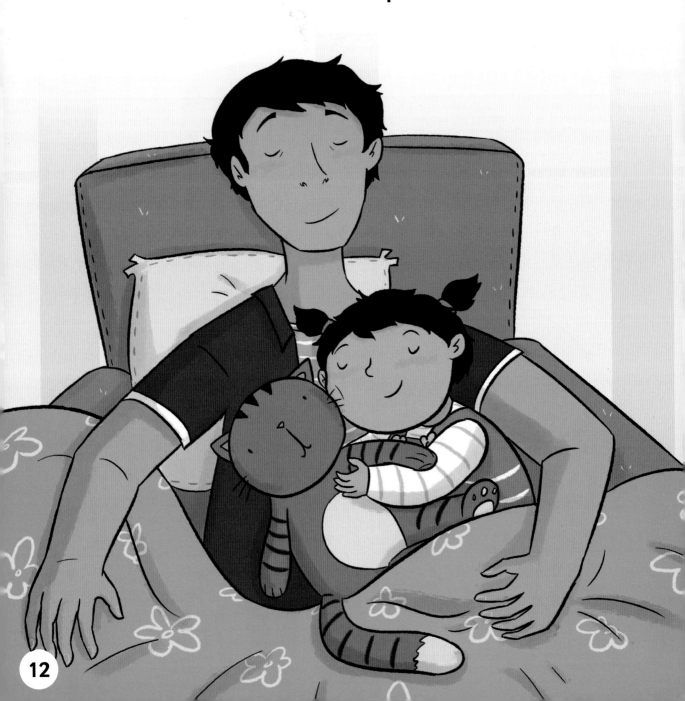